The illustrated guide to
Thames Sailing Barges
2013 edition

ISBN 978-0-9563059-5-4
By Rita and Peter Phillips
who have asserted their rights under the
Copyright, Designs and Patents Act, 1988
to be identified as authors of this work.

Published by Phillips Design Publishing
Tollesbury
phillipsdesignpublishing.co.uk
© All photographs Copyright Phillips Design unless otherwise stated

GW00778030

Printed by Think Ink of Ipswich

Contents

Introduction

Welcome to the 2013 edition of The illustrated guide to Thames Sailing Barges. In this issue we bring you the essential information on all the Thames sailing barges we expect to see sailing this year. This information includes:

- Date and place of launch.
- Port of registration.
- Type of construction.
- Length and Beam.
- Kind of rig, bowsprit or staysail.
- Aids to identification, e.g. Bob colour, sprit banding etc.
- National Historic Ships Certificate Number.
- Brief history.
- Present operator and usual base.
- If listed as a "Dunkirk Little Ship".
- Web sites if appropriate (checked for operation January 2013).
- Barge Matches taken part in last season.
- Colour photograph.

As last year, we have included a section "Barges not currently active" sub divided into "Static examples" and "Work in progress". This is hopefully self-explanatory. Please note that barges can, and frequently do, move between categories over the course of the year and it is quite possible for a barge listed as "Work in Progress" to emerge over the summer. Likewise "Active" barges may not be seen sailing for various reasons. A good example of this latter was *Defiance* last year which did not after all sail as she required further work.

Fertile has been moved from "Active" to "Static" for this season as it is not the owners intention to sail her. He is of course free to change his mind!

Coverage of the Barge Matches has been expanded as they represent the best way of enjoying the sight of a number of barges in close proximity. We also feel that this is an entertaining and worthwhile sport in it's own right. The Sailing Barge Association is endeavouring to raise the profile of these events and we can only hope that the media can be persuaded to give better coverage.

To further stimulate interest in these Matches we have given full details of each barge's participation in last years events. This does not of course guarantee that they will attend the same races this year.

In a change from last year we have included the barge yacht *Dinah* in our main section as she was a Barge Match competitor last year and it would seem inappropriate therefore not to include her. For reasons of space, we cannot list all of the barge yachts individually, especially given the number of "New Builds" coming on the scene. They are however touched upon in our "Other vessels of interest" page.

The main change in this years publication is the addition of a section covering the basic forms of Fishing Smacks to be seen around the East Coast and particularly those involved in Smack Racing. Whilst it is not our intention to cover the subject in depth in this publication, we do feel that their inclusion will be of interest to our readers.

Looking back over the previous twelve months, it was generally a good year, with, as listed in last years edition, a significant number of barges taking part in the Jubilee "Avenue of Sail" - not that you would have known it from the media coverage.

2012 also saw the return of *Niagara* and *Thalatta* to sailing. The latter, not normally a racing barge, taking part in the Thames Match thus, with *Cambria* present, giving the splendid sight of two large "Mulie" barges competing against each other once more.

One of the highlights of the season was to see *Pudge* back to service with the Thames Sailing Barge Trust once more following her refurbishment. Their *Centaur* is scheduled to have major work carried out this year so although listed as "Active" her appearances may be restricted.

Of the "Static" community", *Vigilant*, after many years at St. Osyth made her way, with some help, down to Devon where she is to be restored. *Tollesbury* made her way to Faversham for work and then returned to Barking where no doubt, her return to activity will continue at a leisurely pace, as does the work on *George Smeed* at Maldon.

Probably the outstanding piece of good news is what appears to be the success of the campaign to secure a permanent and secure home for the restoration of *Westmorland* at Faversham.

With the number of restoration projects ongoing there is certainly cause for continued optimism about the future of the Thames barges and of the skills required to keep them alive. The number of these projects which have made little or no progress over recent years is however, testament to the realities of life in our present economic climate.

Sadly, the last twelve months has seen the loss of some well known characters on the barging scene. Of those relevant to this book, Mark Boyle is mentioned in relation to the Thames Match, while Joe Brannigan will be familiar to anyone who has followed the refurbishment of *Thalatta.*

Barge operators generally are of course having to operate in poor financial conditions with maintenance costs continuing to rise and downward pressure on the prices they are able to charge. Charities are in a slightly better position in that they can take advantage of various forms of funding and the Historic Lottery Fund is a godsend when it comes to major work providing applications are meticulously prepared. Life for commercial and private operators remains challenging however as the number of barges currently for sale shows. Last years weather was no help at all!

Despite the economic doom and gloom, most operators seem to be coping and to be reasonably optimistic about the future provided the economy eventually picks up and the sun decides to shine this season!

Rita and Peter Phillips

The role of the Thames sailing barge

By "Thames sailing barge" we mean the flat bottomed cargo carrying craft with spritsail or ketch rigs and lee boards, which have evolved around the Thames, from Kent to Suffolk, for use in the marshes, estuaries, creeks and coastal waters of the area.

The Thames sailing barges we see today have been evolving since the Middle Ages and, through their various uses as training vessels, private yachts and corporate hospitality centres, continue to evolve, though their cargos are now usually people not goods.

The small single masted spritsail rigged vessels common on the Thames in the Middle Ages grew in size and complexity. Bow and stern shapes evolved from their early flat shovel like forms as seen on lighters, to the transom sterns and vertical stems we are familiar with. Mizzen masts were an early addition and from the late Nineteenth Century, tillers began to be replaced by wheels.

The large coasters such as *Cambria, Hydrogen, Thalatta and Will* owe their origins in part to the schooners and ketches working our coastal waters. Indeed the sail plans of the early coasting barges were those of their forefathers.

By the late Nineteenth Century payloads of up to 200 tons were commonplace encompassing every imaginable cargo. Coal from from the North East with a return load of wheat or potatoes, chemicals from the EDME factory at Mistley or munitions from the powder mills on the river Lea. The farm produce of the day would usually travel to the mill or market by barge. Even the sea walls from Kent to Suffolk were built from stone transported by the barges.

One barge could carry enough bricks to build two semi detached houses and fleets were operated by the brick makers. Cross channel trips were also commonplace for the barge fleet, voyages being made to Continental ports with goods as varied as timber or beans, pig iron or cement.

Some of the most important cargos carried were those of straw and grain taken from East Anglia to London to feed the Capital's horse drawn transport system. The return trip was made with a cargo of the recycled product to be used as fertiliser for the regions farms - the "London mixture".

The Thames barge continued to evolve, metal hulls, lighter than wood and without the need for internal bracing gave greater efficiency. Sails were gradually augmented by, then replaced with motors in an attempt to compete with other forms of transport. The growth of the rail and road networks eroded trade for the barges, whatever their power, so that by the 1960's the day of the sailing barge as a cargo carrier had well and truly passed.

In their heyday, from the late Eighteenth Century to the early Twentieth Century the sailing barge was the usual mode of transport for anything needing to be taken to or from the Capital or from farm to mill. The growth of London, the Nation and Empire's economy and infrastructure depended as much on the humble Thames sailing barge as the mighty "Ships of the Line".

The story has not ended and the remaining barges are far from mere historical artefacts.The standard of workmanship, materials, internal design and equipment of the recent renovations has been such as to ensure that they have useful lives in their new roles into the Twenty Second Century.

Notes on barge rigs

These brief notes cover some of the rigs and sail plans used on Thames sailing barges. It is a subject which could easily fill a book in its own right!

Spritsail "Sprittie"

Carrying a sprit on main and mizzen masts, rather than gaff and booms. The sprit rig is recorded back to the middle ages and is ideal for working the sheltered waters of rivers and estuaries. It is economic because it can be worked by only a skipper, mate, and if necessary a third hand. Most of the barges featured in this book are "Spritties"

Ketch or "Boomie"

Gaff and boom main and mizzen masts, often with a fixed bowsprit. Considered by many to be a better rig for open sea work though a crew up to six could be needed making it more expensive to operate. "Boomies" owe their lineage to the sea going schooners and coasters. There are no Thames barges currently carrying this rig though some Dutch barges still use it.

A marriage of the above produced perhaps the pinnacle of barge rigs-

"Mulie"

Often used on the larger coasting barges, it consists of a spritsail rigged main mast with a ketch rigged mizzen, "mulie" being a cross between two rigs! This rig gives a greater total sail area allowing a smaller mains'l and sprit to be carried, making it an easier set up to manage in open water and high winds. *Cambria, Hydrogen, Thalatta* and *Will* are "Mulies."

Whatever the main sail plan there are other variations too-

Bowsprit rig

Where there is a bowsprit extending forward of the stem supporting the sails forward of the main mast. The bowsprit can usually be raised when space is short such as in port or busy areas.

Staysail rig

Where no bowsprit is carried. Traditionally in the rivers and estuaries where greater sail area was less important than the ability to work in confined areas.

"Stumpie"

Where no topmast is carried. *Nellie* is a good example in the current fleet.

"Stackie"

A name given to a barge carrying a cargo of straw or wood partly stacked on deck. Mainsails were frequently brailed up to clear this stack. Barges built to be used as "stackies" were often slightly broader in the beam, as with *Dawn*.

Barges specialising in carrying cargos of bricks were known as "Brickies".

Motor Barge

Many Thames barges were converted to motor barges, some retaining gear to aid loading/unloading or mizzens to help with handling at sea.

Motor Auxiliary or Auxiliary Ketch

As used here, when a motor is fitted but some sails are retained for use.

Note. Many references such as the Merchant Navy Lists, do not differentiate between spritsail and "mulie" rigs.

A very detailed exposition on this subject can be found in *Sailing craft of East Anglia by R Finch and H Benham.* see bibliography.

ADIEU of Harwich

Bob - Plain light blue. Green trim to gunwale. Black sprit with thin white band.

Adieu was built of steel in 1929 by Horlock's for F W Horlock & Co Ltd, a sister ship to *Portlight, Xylonite, Reminder* and *Repertor.* She served with this company through most of her trading life.

Converted to a motor barge in 1949 and laid up as a lighter in 1967, she gradually became a rusting hulk like so many of her breed.

Bought by James Stewart in 1985, her "wafer thin" bottom was renewed by James and Stone. Restoration continued until 1993 and included a new lining, mast and rigging, the permanent sheeting of her holds, a new aft deck, the complete replacement of all deck gear (except the main horse) and many other details.

Owned and Iolo Brooks, *Adieu* is now operated as a barge yacht from St Katharine's Dock. She has the distinction of being one of the last sailing barges to be worked on at the Old Dolphin Yard at Sittingbourne when she had her sails dressed there.

Usually competing in several barge matches over a season, in 2012 *Adieu* only competed in the Thames Match where she has been a regular competitor over the years. She is seen here making the most of the early dull but breezy conditions, she finished third in the "Champion Bowsprit" class.

ALICE of Rochester

Staysail Class   *SSR No 68024*

Photo courtesy Alan Gick

Bob - Blue G on yellow ground. Cream sprit with white/green/white banding.
Length 77 ft. Beam 18 ft.

Alice was built as a steel swim head lighter by J W Cook for Hubbocks, for whom she operated from the river Lea to the Lower Pool of London. During this time she operated as a lighter and was, for a short time in the 1970's, used to supply the Pirate Radio station "Radio Caroline". She was taken out of trade in 1994.

Bought by Owen Emersen, he undertook very extensive work over the next three years. In 1998, with a refashioned bow and stern, all the necessary sailing equipment, an engine and a fully fitted pine interior *Alice* was re-commissioned as a classic Thames sailing barge.

Owned since 2005 by the Gick family, *Alice* operates in the Solent from Gun Wharf Quays, Portsmouth. She is able to accommodate up to 40 people alongside the quay or 12 when sailing. Stag and Hen parties and weekend cruises make up about 65% of her charters.

Owner Alan Gick reports a fairly good season for 2012 citing the benefits of open water close at hand in the Solent and easy access.

Antifouling over Christmas 2012 produced the unusual sight of a Thames barge being craned out of the water and transported by land on a cradle to the yard where the work was done!

www.alice4-charter.co.uk
Ring for bookings 07979751433

ARDWINA of London

Bob - Red 'A' & navigational dividers on 3 blue horizontal bands on white ground. Has "Rolfe Judd" in topsail. Plain brown sprit. Length 85 ft. Beam 21.1 ft.

The last wooden barge built by Orvis and Fuller at Ipswich, *Ardwina* was launched in 1909, spending most of her working life in general trade on the East Coast. She was owned by Goldsmith's of London until 1938, when, having lost her mast, she was abandoned at sea, being recovered by Ocean Salvage after three days.

Ardwina passed to Metcalf Motor Coasters in the same year and on to Daniels Bros. In 1951. *Ardwina* was reported as carrying cargos of Portland stone from Dorset to London in 1959, shortly before she came out of trade.

Ardwina has had a number of owners and refurbishments, spending some time as a houseboat. She had a major refit at David Patient's yard at Maldon in 1989/90, where she had further work carried out in early 2011.

Ardwina has been owned and operated since 1980 by Ardwina Ltd as a charter and hospitality barge for Rolfe Judd and Co, a firm of London Architects.

In addition to her work on "the London River" *Ardwina* is usually an active member of the racing fraternity. Competing in the Passage, Pin Mill and Black-water events in 2012, she finished tenth in the Thames Barge championship.

Over the winter of 2012/3 *Ardwina* had her standing rigging removed, inspected and serviced by Jim Dines and his team at Maldon. The same team who re-rigged the *Cutty Sark*.

www.ardwina.co.uk

CABBY of Rochester

Bowsprit Class   Official No. 160687   NHSR Core Collection Cert. No. 134

Bob - Plain white C on plain red ground. Dark grey lower hull with black wale. Plain brown sprit. Length 91.93 ft. Beam 21.5 ft. Dunkirk Little Ship.

The last full size barge built of wood at Rochester, *Cabby* was constructed by Gill for the London & Rochester Barge Company. Work started in 1925 but because of the economic climate at the time she was not completed until three years later.

In 1940, when at Ipswich, she was ordered to Dunkirk with drums of freshwater for the troops. Redirected to Brest, she was finally ordered to Plymouth without reaching France! Subsequent war service saw her visit Ireland, the Clyde and the Hebrides where she was given a new wheelhouse.

After the war, as a motor barge, *Cabby* carried cargos such as cement, china clay and Portland stone travelling as far afield as Antwerp. Finishing cargo work in the late 1960's, *Cabby* worked on as a passenger carrier before being re-rigged in 1970 and used as a company charter barge. Since this time *Cabby* has had several owners, currently Sailing Barge Cabby Ltd of Maylandsea.

Cabby operates as a corporate venue and charter barge on the river Thames.

Entering the occasional Barge Match she took part in the Blackwater and Swale events in 2012, winning the "Restricted Staysail" class in the latter (without using her bowsprit!) and finishing fourteenth in the over all Championship.

www.sailingbargecabby.co.uk

CAMBRIA of London

Bowsprit class   *Official number 120676*

Bob - Red, white, blue and green quadrants. Length 90.95 ft. Beam 22 ft.

Built of wood by William Everard of Greenhithe in 1906, *Cambria* was a sister barge to the *Hibernia*, built by William's brother Frederick at the same time. *Cambria* spent much of her early working life doing cross channel trips with cargoes included pitch, coke, wheat and oil cake. She also built a reputation as a fine racing barge. *Cambria* remained with Everard's until sold off to Bob Roberts who operated her from 1966 to 1970.

Cambria, now owned by The Maritime Trust as part of their "Historic Ship Collection" moved to St. Katharine's Dock as a museum ship in 1971.

In 1987 badly in need of restoration, she was sold to the Cambria Trust for £1 and towed to Dolphin yard at Sittingbourne.

An HLF grant helped restoration work to be carried out under the leadership of Tim Goldsack at Faversham. This work, which included the fitting of stream-lined "racing" lee boards, was completed in time for *Cambria* to sail again in 2011, since when she has been used as a "Floating Classroom".

Competing in the Medway, Thames and Colne Barge Matches in 2012, she finished first in her class in each one! These excellent results were enough to see her secure sixth place over all in the Championship.

"Mulie" rigged, *Cambria* now sports the distinctive Rotarian "wheel" logo in her tops'l. Further work carried out over winter, including to the plumbing and waste system, should now see *Cambria* in better shape than ever.

www.cambriatrust.org.uk

CENTAUR of Harwich

Bob - Gold wheel on red & black ground. Cream sprit with black, cream and red banding. Length 85.54 ft. Beam 19.5 ft.

Built of wood at Harwich in 1895 by John and Herbert Cann, *Centaur* was originally owned by Charles Stone. She passed through several owners including Edward Hibbs of Brightlinsea for whom she was listed in 1916, John Sawyer (MNL 1934) and Francis Gilder (MNL 1938) before going to the London & Rochester Trading Company.

1944 saw her in the service of Brown and Co. who had her de-rigged and employed as a timber lighter.

Centaur was bought in 1966 by Richard Duke who re-rigged her and used her as a charter barge before selling her in 1974 to the Thames Barge Sailing Club (now Trust) for members sailing.

Based at Maldon and rebuilt 1984-95, *Centaur* continues to be operated by the Thames Sailing Barge Trust along with *S B Pudge*. TSBT is an organisation dedicated to promoting and teaching the practice of the traditional skills of seamanship involved in sailing and maintaining these historic craft.

Centaur only competed in the Pin Mill Match in 2012, winning "Class C" this being enough to give her seventeenth position in the Barge Championship.

Seen above following the Colne Match above, opportunities to see *Centaur* sailing may be limited in the coming year as she is scheduled for major refurbishment work .

www.bargetrust.org

CYGNET of Harwich

Bob - Plain red. Plain brown sprit. Length 41.96 ft. Beam 12.98 ft.

A half size, genuine working barge *Cygnet* was built of wood in 1881 by Curel for use trading to small farm creeks. Originally owned by Walter Wrinch of Ewarton, near Shotley, she stayed in family ownership carrying farm produce round the Suffolk area until 1945. For the next ten years *Cygnet* enjoyed a complete change of role, when, bought by a Mr E Mumford she had her sailing gear replaced by two petrol engines and she moved to Foulness carrying cockle shells for chicken grit.

Subsequently having owners at Leigh on Sea and Queenborough and with duties including acting as a supply vessel, *Cygnet* passed to her present owner Mica Brown in 1988, who refitted her as a private yacht barge and bases her at Snape Maltings, from where she is sailed single handed by Des Kaliszewski.

Cygnet has her mizzen stepped on her rudder post and in 2004 acquired a tiller rather than a wheel for steering, both shown to good effect in the photo above, taken at the Colne Match of 2011.

Cygnet caused quite a stir a few years ago when sailing the East Coast with a stack of straw stowed on her deck in traditional manner, a sight not seen for many years and not seen again until *Dawn* featured in the *Lost routes of Britain* programme in the summer of 2012.

Having attended the Jubilee "Avenue of Sail" in June last year *Cygnet* also competed in the Pin Mill Barge Match where her one point earned her equal twenty first place in the overall Championship.

DAWN of Maldon

Bowsprit Class   *Official No. 105902*   *NHSR Cert. No. 221*

Bob - Plain dark blue. Cream gunwale. Plain cream sprit. Length 81.9 ft. Beam 20 ft. Dunkirk Little Ship.

Dawn was built of wood as a "Stackie" in 1897 by Walter Cook of Maldon for James Keeble. She was sold to Joshua Francis in 1933 then operated by Francis and Gilder's.

Commandeered at the start of WW2 and ordered to Dunkirk, *Dawn* was hit by an Admiralty tug in Dover Harbour and had to return to Maldon for repairs instead. She is however listed by A.D.L.S. as a "Dunkirk Little Ship".

Becoming a motor barge and then a lighter, *Dawn* was rescued by Gordon Swift in 1967 and re-rigged and used as a charter barge from Maldon. 1978 saw her with the Passmore Edwards Museum of Newham who used her for children's trips, still under the same Captain.

There followed a period of disuse and general deterioration until she was rescued by the formation of the "Dawn Sailing Barge Trust" who, with the help of the Heritage Lottery Fund completed her restoration at Heybridge in 2008.

One of the highlights of 2012 was the broadcasting of the superb TV programme in the *Lost Routs of Britain* series. *Dawn* was shown taking a stack of straw from Salcott creek to St Katherine's dock on the Thames, thus recreating a common voyage in the early Twentieth Century.

Not a Barge Match competitor last year *Dawn* advertises a busy schedule of weekend and evening cruises in 2013 from her West Mersea base *(above)*.

www.dawn-trust.org.uk

DECIMA of London

White gunwale. Black sprit with blue/yellow/blue banding. Length 85 ft. Beam 19.6 ft.

Decima (A Roman Goddess, one of the fates) was built of steel by Fay at Southampton in 1899, for E J & W Goldsmith Ltd of Grays. She continued to carry general cargo for this owner until the late 1940's when she was sold to Rayfields at Gravesend. Adventures included being abandoned by her crew in a gale off Great Yarmouth and sailing herself safely to Holland in 1938 and being swamped and sunk at anchor off Southend Pier in 1940. (It's probably a coincidence that she has not competed in the Southend Match recently)!

In the 1960's she was converted to a motor barge and went to Greenhithe Lighterage Co. Ltd. *Decima* was re-rigged as a sailing barge when she left trade in 1977, being bought by Dennis Wildish who operated her thus for some years. Sold in 1996 she was used as a houseboat on Faversham creek.

Decima's fortunes were to take a turn for the better when she was purchased by Tim Goldsack in 2003 who carried out extensive replacement of her hull and deck plates, together with fitting a new Gardner engine and replacing much of her sailing gear.

Having secured sponsorship from Tiptree Jams, *Decima* now sports their logo in her tops'l as seen in the photo above taken at last years Colne Match. In 2012 *Decima* competed in all except the Passage, Thames and Southend Matches and finished equal seventh overall.

www.sailingbargecharterdecima.com

15

DEFIANCE of London

Photo courtesy Phillip Apps

Bob - Yellow crescent, red sun yellow star within, on a blue background with red ends. Cream sprit with broad blue band. Length 78 ft. Beam 17.8 ft.

Built by Lambon Hull Ltd, of Rushock, Worcestershire, *Defiance* left there in March 2008. She was taken on a low loader to Tilbury, where she was launched by crane and tugged round to Allington Lock, Maidstone. At this time *Defiance* was only a hull with a Gardner engine in situ.

Owner Philip Apps spent the next two years working on her, *Defiance* also spent a year at Stargate Marina where she was shortened by 300 mm. Major adjustments were also made to gain more run on the bow and stern. Having made four knots under full power when she left Allington Lock and making just under ten on way back,the modifications must have worked!

Defiance is built on the lines of a River Barge, with not much sheer, as can be seen in the photo above, taken at her Allington Lock base. She was named after the Hudson's of Maidstone built *Defiance* (Off. No 26241) of 1789.

Some of her equipment has been "recycled" from other barges. Steering gear from *Lady Helen,* wheel, windless and lee boards from *Jock,* main brail winch from *Felix,* some rigging from *Dawn* and a top cap from *Niagara!*

It is planned to use *Defiance* as a barge yacht and she is fitted out for living aboard.

Further work on the rigging meant that *Defiance* was not after all, ready to sail in the 2012 season. It is anticipated that she will move to Hoo before the Medway match which she plans to attend.

DINAH of Rochester

Official No. 090995

Bob -Red and White. Red trim fore and aft. Length 45 ft. Beam 12 ft.

Dinah was built by Gill and sons of Rochester in 1887 as a 45 ft barge yacht for The Hon. Reginald Brougham, inventor of the metal golf wood.

Originally spritsail rigged she certainly remained so in 1916 when she is shown as such in the MNL of that year, being shown as in the service of Howard Hollingsworth of North Lowestoft.

Dinah is said to have been subsequently converted to a gaff rig and certainly had a tall mainmast and topmast with a standing gaff and no bowsprit when she was taken to Whitehouse Boatyard at Hoo in 1947. Major work was undertaken including replacing her old paraffin engine with a Ford V8 unit.

In 1979 Aidan de la Mare rescued her from a lighter in Gloucester where she had become derelict. *Dinah* was taken to Dock End Yard in Ipswich where major refurbishment work was started but not finished.

In 2003 Richard Johnson had her totally restored in Southwold by a traditional boat builder. Three years of work on the restoration was aided by three generations – Grandfather 84, son 50 and grandson 20 years old.

Dinah has now been fully restored and operates from Iken Barns in Suffolk. Usually occupied doing River Cruises, she is seen here following the 2011 Pin Mill Match, the only event in which she competed in 2012.

www.ikenbarns.com/barge-sailing.html

EDITH MAY of Harwich

Staysail class   *Official Number 116180*

Bob - light blue, with a dark blue circle containing a wheat sheaf.
Length 86 ft. Beam 20.75 ft.

Built of wood by J & H Cann of Harwich in 1906. *Edith May* was spritsail rigged from the beginning, with a Ford Diesel engine. She spent her early life working the East Coast carrying grain, though cargos of ammunition from Felixstowe to Norfolk are also reported in the Autumn 2010 edition of the magazine "Mainsheet" from SSBR.

Edith May spent time with Wm. J Barrette, for whom she appears in the 1916 MNL and for Alfred Sully of London in the 1930's. After WW 2, like many of her kind she was converted to a motor barge and operated as such until 1961.

Re-rigged by Vernon Harvey she became a successful racing barge. Sold, she went to Liverpool in 1980. Moving to St Katharine's Dock in 1990.

In 1999, *Edith May* was bought, in a dilapidated condition, by her present owners and moved to Lower Halstow where a magnificent restoration was carried out concluding with her re-launch on June 18 2010.

2012 saw *Edith May's* most successful season to date, attending the Jubilee Festival and finishing as Champion Barge having competed in all except the Swale Barge Matches. She is seen finishing the Colne Match.

This year will again be a busy year as attendance at both the Rochester Sweeps Festival and the Dickens Festival are scheduled together with all except the Blackwater Barge Matches.

www.edithmay.com

Bob - White 'H' on red ground. White 'EDME' in topsail. Plain cream sprit.
Length 80 ft. Beam 17.25 ft.

Built of wood by J & H Cann at Harwich in 1898 for F W Horlock. Named after the English Diastatic Malt Extract Company (which still operates in Mistley). *Edme* continued in trade under sail until 1949 when she was de-rigged and used as a lighter by Brown and Co. When her days as a lighter were over, *Edme* underwent a lengthy period of restoration at Maldon before being bought by the Harman-Harrison Consortium in 1989.

In 2002 the EDME company sponsored a new tops'l for *Edme* and commissioned her to carry flour from Mistley Quay to Greens Flour Mill in Maldon, the first time a Thames sailing barge had carried such a cargo since the 1970's.

Based at Skipper Andy Harman's boat yard at St. Osyth, she is used for charter work out of Brightlingsea having a sailing capacity of twelve passengers.

2012 saw *Edme* compete in all except the Passage, Thames and Southend Matches finishing third over all in the Championship. *Edme* had a distinguished guest on board for the Thames Match playing host to the popular TV personality Griff Rhys Jones a keen barge supporter and presenter of programmes featuring *Lady of the Lea* and, more recently, *Dawn*.

Proudly boasting of being one of the few remaining engineless barges, *Edme's* shallow draft is apparent in this view of her in the Medway Match. She has had remedial work done to her starboard chine over the winter.

www.edmebarge.com

ETHEL ADA of London

Staysail Class Official No 118352 *NHSR Cert. No. 200*

Bob - Green with white circle. Cream sprit with blue/white/blue/white bands.
Length 80 ft. Beam 20.49 ft.

Ethel Ada was built of wood in 1903 at Pagglesham by the Shuttlewood brothers and is said to be named after their two wives. Having been built in the same creek as Charles Darwin's *Beagle,* legend has it that she is constructed from some of that vessel's timbers!

Ethel Ada worked for a number of owners including G and A Underwood Coal Merchants, Samual West Ltd of London, for whom she is listed in 1916 and 1934, carrying ballast, T F Wood and later I.C.I. Ltd carrying explosives.

Passing into private use at the end of her trading career in the 1960's, *Ethel Ada* was given an engine in the 1980's. Having spent some time in the rural splendor of first Pin Mill and then Snape, she now earns her living on the "London river" as a charter barge operating from St Katherine's or Hermitage Wharf. She did make a return visit to Snape in late summer 2009 where she was another attractive feature at this Suffolk beauty spot.

Ethel Ada has not competed in Barge Matches since 2010 when she is pictured here. Currently for sale at £150k, (her London berth is separately for sale), it is unlikely that she will be competing in the near future and her charter work will probably be very limited.

Despite the prospect of a fairly quiet summer, *Ethel Ada* should be receiving a new rudder in the spring of 2013.

www.ethel-ada.co.uk/charters

GLADYS of Harwich

Bowsprit Class   *Official No. 109882*   *NHSR Cert. No. 204*

Bob - Green, orange & gold triangular. 'Kingsmill' emblem in topsail. Plain cream sprit
Length 84 ft. Beam 20.6 ft.

Built by Cann of Harwich, of wood in 1901, last of at least four barges to carry the name *Gladys* (not all by the same builder). Her first owners were William Thomas Whitmore of Harwich (master mariner with 48 shares) and John Howard (master mariner with 16 shares) of Shoeburyness. *Gladys* was sold to John Lesley Whitemore of Lancashire a year later though John Howard remained as master.

Gladys passed to Cranfield Brothers Ltd, with Charles Howard as the master, in 1912. She stayed with this company most of her life. In 1950 a diesel engine was fitted and she was re-registered.

Passing to Mardorf Peach Ltd in the early 1970's she was re-rigged and served as a company yacht, a role she still fulfils today.

Gladys was acquired by her present owners, Allied Mills in 1999 and fitted with a new transom in 2003. She continues as a company hospitality vessel based at St. Katharine's Dock being used from May to September for river trips, training days and conferences for her owners.

Gladys usually spends her winters at Heybridge Basin where she is pictured in the early winter of 2012. She did not compete in any of the Barge Matches last year and is probably best viewed on the "London River".

www.sailingbargegladys.co.uk

GRETA of Colchester

Staysail Class   *Official No. 9832*   *NHSR Cert. No. 206*

Bob - Red N on black & gold ground. Topsail has white Shepherds crook and mainsail has white 'SHEPHERD NEAME, BREWER, FAVERSHAM Sprit cream with Light Blue band trimmed with Dark Blue. Length 80 ft. Beam 20 ft. Dunkirk Little Ship.

Built of wood by Stone of Brightlingsea in 1892 for a sail maker named Hibbs. *Greta* passed from Hibbs to the fleet of Owen Parry, where she usually carried such cargo as grain and malt. A notable exception was when she carried the spars for the Kaiser's racing schooner!

Greta was sold to the London Rochester Barge Company in 1918. Passing out of trade in the 1960's, *Greta* was converted to a houseboat and re-rigged, having become a motor barge in 1951.

Greta is said to be the oldest active barge to have taken part in the Dunkirk evacuation and took part in the 60th anniversary celebrations, Prince Charles coming aboard to speak with Skipper/owner Steve Norris. In 2008 a grant was received from National Historic Ships for the replacement of her fore and aft main hatches. In September 2009 she delivered a cargo of Shepherd and Neame's beer to St Katharine's Dock for the London Festival, the barrels being unloaded using her sprit as a derrick.

Greta, seen here at her Whitstable base, is a busy charter barge so sadly cannot attend many Barge Matches, only attending the Whitstable Festival and Swale Match in 2012. She undergoes regular maintenance work with the next major project being a new side to her hull.

www.greta1892.co.uk

HYDROGEN of London

Bob - Green, red & white. Plain brown sprit. Length 94.75 ft. Beam 24.49 ft.

Built of wood in 1906 by Gills of Rochester to carry tar and oil, *Hydrogen* had her tanks for these removed in 1910 when she was sold to G Andrews who used her for general cargo work. During this time she would carry cement up to the Humber, returning to the Thames and Medway rivers with coal.

At some time between 1934 and 1938 ownership passed from G to H Andrews and her original ketch rig was changed to Sprits'l. She passed to G F Sully and was commandeered in 1941. She did her war service on the Clyde.

After the war she returned to trade, operating until 1976 as a motor rather than sailing barge. *Hydrogen* was purchased by Bells whisky in 1978 for whom she became a well known sight round the UK coast, entertaining many of her owners guests in ports en-route. For this work she was returned to sail as a "mulie".

Bought by the Blackwater Barge Co. in 1992, *Hydrogen* is now used as a charter barge out of Maldon. As such she is the largest wooden barge still sailing. "Mulie" rigged she claims to have the "Tallest mizzen in the fleet"!

Operated by Topsail Charters Ltd, she had a busy 2012 carrying up to fifty passengers on charters. She is usually to be seen fully laden following the Barge Matches as illustrated above when she took advantage of a rare sunny day at the Colne Match of 2012.

www.top-sail.co.uk

KITTY of Harwich

Bob - White star on red ground. White star in topsail. Green hull. Cream sprit with green band. Length 82.13 ft. Beam 19.38 ft.

Kitty was built of wood in 1895 by J H Cann of Harwich for Horlock's as part of their fleet of grain carriers. In WW1 she carried out the dangerous task of transporting stores across the channel to Calais and Boulogne.

Francis & Gilders bought *Kitty* in 1938 later passing her on to the London and Rochester Trading Company who continued to employ her in trade until selling her on to Brown and Co. who used her as a timber lighter.

1964/5 saw *Kitty's* prospects improve when she was bought by Maldon Yacht and Barge Charter Ltd and re-rigged as a charter vessel.

Becoming a notable racing barge *Kitty* eventually changed owners in 1976 being de rigged and becoming a floating restaurant at Hayling Island. In 1985 she was purchased by Patrick Keen of Portsmouth, re rigged and a Perkins diesel engine fitted. She was also re named *My Kitty*.

A further change of ownership took place in 1988 and again in 1990 when she passed to Roger Marriott who operated her as a charter barge out of Port Solent and then Southampton. By now her name had reverted to *Kitty*.

Although put up for sale in 2008, *Kitty* moved up to Maldon that year and is operated and chartered by Topsail Charters of Maldon. As a charter barge *Kitty* is licensed to carry up to 40 passengers and reports a very busy 2012 cruising the Blackwater as seen above, or following the local Barge Matches.

www.top-sail.co.uk

LADY DAPHNE of Rochester

Staysail Class   *Official No. 127276*   *NHSR Cert. No. 210*

Bob - blue and red .White Z in topsail. Plain cream sprit.
Length 90.8 ft. Beam 21.4 ft.

Built of wood in 1923 by Short Bros. of Rochester for David J Bradley for whose family *Lady Daphne* continued to trade until joining the fleet of R & W Paul (Maltsters) Ltd of Ipswich in 1937.

Having been first fitted with an engine in 1932, *Lady Daphne* was re-engined with a Ruston and Hornsby five cylinder motor in 1947. Some ten years later sail gave way to power completely and she operated as a motor barge until sold to Taylor Woodrow Property Ltd in 1973. New owners meant a new lease of life as *Lady Daphne* was re-rigged for charter and promotional work.

In 1996 ownership passed to Elisabeth and Michael Mainelli who operate her under the banner of Nymph Ltd as a corporate entertainment and charter barge. Carrying fifty five passengers, She usually sails from St. Katharine's Dock.

The winter of 2009/10 saw an overhaul of *Lady Daphne's* steering gear at Faversham. In 2011 she had a new midship section, portside framing and planking and starboard side wale replaced. She also had upgrades including improvements to the galley, heads and focs'l. Further work was carried out in 2012, particularly to the galley and heads.

Repair work following a collision at the Pin Mill Match limited *Lady Daphne's* appearances to just that one event, but it is hoped to attend at least the Thames Match in 2013. She is currently for sale at £175k.

www.lady-daphne.co.uk

LADY OF THE LEA of Dover

Bowsprit Class *Official No. 722956* *NHSR Cert. No. 212*

Bob - plain red. Has white barge inside castle, all inside double circle emblem in topsail Dark brown sprit with grey band. Length 72 ft. Beam 13 ft.

Built of wood in 1931 by Hyam & Oliver at Rotherhithe as a "War Department Sailing Barge", her early duties were to carry armaments between Waltham Abbey and Woolwich Arsenal. She was the last sailing barge to be built following the plans of canal barges from a century earlier and originally had tiller steering and was stumpy rigged. To deal with her part open river and part canal journeys she was often powered by horse as well as sail!

The Royal Gunpowder Mills at Waltham Abbey have a diorama showing *Lady of the Lea* at work when she would have loaded 500 barrels of gunpowder each cargo. She returned to the River Lea in the Autumn of 2009 being featured on a BBC Television programme on the area.

A petrol engine was added by the Navy in 1943, to be replaced by a diesel in 1980. She was sold to W Aslett in 1946 and subsequently to her present owner Brian Pain. She was largely rebuilt between 1980 and 1990 including doubling her bottom and lower hull. She is now based at Standard Quay Faversham.

Lady of the Lea added to her TV credits in 2012 appearing on the BBC2 series "Our Food" at the beginning of the year. She competed in all the Barge Matches last year winning her class in the Southend Match and gaining a number of "Fastest start"s. She did consistently well enough to finish second over all in the Championship. She is pictured in the Medway Match.

MARJORIE of Ipswich

Bowsprit Class   *Official No. 113753*

Bob - Lemon & black quarters with lemon 'D' & '105' on black quarters. Sprit brown with black and yellow banding. Length 84 ft. Beam 19.3 ft.

Built of wood in 1902 by Orvis in Ipswich, *Marjorie* was owned initially by R & W Paul Ltd sailing as a coastal barge. She continued to trade under sail with the same firm until 1961 when she became a charter barge owned by a Mr A J O'Shea and based at Maldon.

Marjorie continued at Maldon for some time and still occasionally visits for the Blackwater Barge Match.

After a period of ownership by Albert Groom, she passed to barrister Simon Devonshire who had her restored by Robert Deards who also skippers her.

Based at Robert's yard at Hoo or at St Katherine's Dock in London, *Marjorie* sadly suffered collision damage in the Swale Barge Match of 2008 which put her out of action for some months. Happily she was back in action for the 2009 season.

Briefly a Staysail Class barge when her bowsprit was removed following a breakage in 2010, *Marjorie* is now once more complete as can be seen in this picture of her finishing the 2012 Colne Match.

A regular Barge Match competitor, *Marjorie* only missed the Medway and Passage Matches in 2012. Winning the "Bowsprit Class" as well as being "First round the outer mark" in the Southend Match, she finishing fifth over all in the Championship.

MAY of Ipswich

Bowsprit Class   *Official No. 97680*   *NHSR Cert. No. 214*

Bob - Blue and white horizontal stripes. White TATE & LYLE in topsail. Sprit plain cream. Length 80.95 ft. Beam 18.98 ft.

Built of wood in 1891 by Cann of Harwich for Cranfields, the Ipswich millers. *May* spent most of her working life carrying grain from the London Docks to her owner's mills. After WW2 she spent much of her time carrying general cargo until purchased by Silvertown Services Lighterage Ltd (later absorbed by Tate and Lyle), for whom she carried occasional cargos of sugar to the Isle of White and was used to train apprentices, before becoming a hospitality barge.

In 1972, during the dock strike, *May* carried a cargo of Portland stone to London for the renovation of St. Paul's Cathedral.

An unusual claim to fame for a Thames barge was her transportation as cargo to the Canadian Lakes for the 1976 Olympics!

In 2010 *May* received a Sustainability Grant of £2000 for cabin hatchment work from the Strategic Development Fund of National Historic Ships.

May is now owned by Gerald and Connie Gadd and operated through Thames and Orwell Marine Services as a charter barge with a capacity of 40 Passengers. She is usually based at Pin Mill though she operates round the East Coast and from St Katharine's in London. *May* attended the "Avenue of Sail" Jubilee celebrations in June 2012 but did not compete in any Barge Matches.

May is pictured above in the Pin Mill Barge Match of 2011 where she is seen approaching Shotley.

www.sailingbargemay.co.uk.

MELISSA of London

Staysail Class

Official No. 110078

Bob - Red and white horizontal stripes, pale sprit, no banding.
Length 85.3 ft. Beam 19.2 ft.

Built of steel by J G Fay of Southampton in 1899, *Melissa* is a sister ship to *Decima* being one of twenty eight built by the same firm for E J and W Goldsmith. *Melissa* spent most of her early life carrying building materials between the South Coast and London for this firm.

In 1942 *Melissa* was bought by the London and Rochester Trading Company. Two years later she was de-rigged and re-registered as a motor barge with a Bergius diesel engine giving her an estimated speed of 5.5 Knots. She also had a wheelhouse fitted at this time.

Sold in 1951, *Melissa* went through several owners until being sold out of trade as a houseboat in 1975. That might have been the end of the story, as with so many of her kind had she not been bought in 1994 by Jonathan Webb and his father Fred. This dedicated pair set about a complete restoration back to sailing configuration but including two Holland 450/NE engines of 5.0 Litres each. Sadly Fred did not live to see *Melissa's* return to sailing in 2009, when she won the Pin Mill Match in her first competitive sail. Restoration has continued at Pin Mill including a new generator being fitted.

In 2012 Melissa competed in her native Pin Mill Match, the Thames Match where she is pictured above and the Colne Match finishing eleventh overall in the Championship.

www.sbmelissa.co.uk

MIROSA of Maldon

Bowsprit Class   Official No. 96488   NHSR Core Collection. Cert. No. 215

Bob - Lemon Tudor rose on blue ground. Sprit cream with a black band.
Length 82 ft. Beam 20.75 ft.

Built as the spritsail rigged stack barge *Ready* at Maldon in 1892 by John Howard. Originally owned by Charles Gutteridge of Vauxhall and later by W W Keeble, *Ready* was with Charles Pudney in 1934.

By 1938, still a spritsail barge, she had passed to Francis and Gilder who renamed her *Mirosa* in 1947, after Josh Francis wife and daughter. (The name *"Ready"* being sold to Trinity House for £35)! *Mirosa* continued in trade until 1955 when she was used as a timber lighter until being restored with a full set of traditional flax sails and manila running rigging by new, private owners in 1965.

Mirosa is now owned by Peter Dodds and has been based at Iron Wharf, Favesham for the last twenty five years. She is available for corporate chartering and Private Hire for day trips on the Swale.

Mirosa was one of the last barges to earn her living entirely under sail, she has never had an engine fitted and can be seen from time to time being towed up river by a local tug, a sight evocative of earlier days.

Mirosa attended the Pin Mill and Swale Barge Matches in 2012 winning her class and the over all seamanship awards in both events and finishing seventh over all in the Championship.

Above we see *Mirosa* passing Osea Island in the 2010 Blackwater Match.

For Charter information ring 07831 328382 or
www.ironwharf.co.uk/charters

NELLIE of Faversham

Staysail Class   *Official No. 114452*

Bob - Plain emerald green Sprit plain cream.
Length 79.25 ft. Beam 17.5 ft.

Built of wood at Faversham for Charles Cremer, the brick manufacturer, in 1901. *Nellie* was used for river work for most of her life, no doubt transporting many of the ten million bricks a year turned out by her owners.

In 1947 Nellie passed to Daniels Bros. of Whitstable who operated her until she was bought by R Lapthorn & Co. Ltd in 1951 for whom she worked until 1960. When Tony Lapthorn and his son retired the company was sold to new owners who traded as Coastal Bulk Shipping Ltd (which ceased trading in 2008). *Nellie* was operated as a motor barge from 1952.

Coming out of trade, *Nellie* was used for years as a houseboat, before being rebuilt at Twickenham in 1985 and completed by Cooks of Maldon in 1994.

Nellie is now owned by Professor Diane Montgomery, who uses her as a floating home at Maldon. Invited to attend the fiftieth anniversary celebrations for Lapthorn's in 2001 *Nellie* was sponsored for a new mizzen tabernacle to mark the event.

Said to be the last Faversham built sailing barge still in operation her relatively small size and stumpy rig means that she can be sailed single handed.

Recent work has included having her sprit lengthened by twelve feet in 2003 and her rotted wooden mast replaced with a metal one. More sail area is her owners next objective!

The best time to see *Nellie* is when she follows the Blackwater Barge Match.

NIAGARA of London

Bob - Red with a yellow star and 5 bar gate Sprit Plain.
Length 86 ft. Beam 20 ft.

Built of metal by Forrestt at Wivenhoe in 1898. Probably spritsail rigged from the beginning, she certainly was when operated by Tilbury Contracting & Dredging Co. in 1914 as listed in the Merchant Navy List for that year.

Niagara later moved to the London and Rochester Trading Company like so many of her kind being recorded in their service in 1934 and 1938 and probably beyond.

An illustrious career very nearly came to a sad end at Cole Jetty Deptford creek some years ago when present owner Peter Sands was one of those asked to look at her with a view to quoting a price to cut her up for scrap. Fortunately, it was decided that she was in far too good a condition for that!

Eleven years and hundreds of man hours have now elapsed and a transformation has been worked. Tasks completed include new plates to starboard and underneath to replace those damaged when *Niagara* was in a lighter awaiting her fate. A new fors'l and staysail have also been added.

Niagara competed in the Swale, Southend and Colne matches in 2012 winning the Charles Morse Trophy for the best restoration at the Colne event and finishing ninth over all in the Championship.

Not a charter barge, *Niagara* should nonetheless be highly visible this year as it is hoped to enter her in all the Barge Matches in 2013.

ORINOCO of London

Bob - plain dark green Sprit brown with white/black/white banding.
Length 86 ft. Beam 21.5 ft.

Built of wood by Hughes at East Greenwich in 1895 and said to be the last remaining active barge from that area.

Originally owned by Masons the cement makers, *Orinoco* passed to Cranfield Bros, possibly when Masons ceased trading in 1907. In any case, she was listed as Cranfield's in the 1916 and 1938 Merchant Navy Lists. *Orinoco* had a white ball emblem in her tops'l when she went to Cranfield's and the company adopted this as a motif for their fleet!

Orinoco had a long career with this owner who fitted her with a Ruston Auxiliary engine in 1947. Retirement came eventually and, having been run down and sunk in the Thames Estuary in 1966, she was repaired and re-rigged by Chester Lighterage and subsequently operated privately by their owner.

Orinoco ran aground when she dragged her anchor in the storms of 1977. It took six months to re-float her when she was sold. More changes of ownership followed as did a successful racing career.

Bought by her present owner Geoffrey Ingle in 1998, *Orinoco* is now based at Faversham and continues to compete in local Barge Matches from time to time.

In 2012 *Orinoco* only competed in the Swale Match where she was runner up in the "Restricted Staysail" class. She is pictured at the Medway Match of 2011.

PHOENICIAN of London

Staysail Class   *Official No. 146700*   *NHSR Cert. No. 161*

Bob - Blue, gold, red & white. Sprit dark brown with no banding.
Length 79.93 ft. Beam 20 ft.

Built of wood by Wills and Packham at Sittingbourne in 1922 and believed to be the last wooden Thames barge built. *Phoenician's* early owners included E A Horlock and R Sulley, who she was listed with in the 1934 and 1938 Merchant Navy Lists. Said to have been built partially for racing, she was a very successful competitor in pre war Barge Matches.

In June 1940 *Phoenician* was badly damaged when an aircraft crashed into the East Anglia Flour Mill at Felixstowe Docks. Repaired, she went to the Walton Backwaters for the unglamorous but vital job of mooring barrage balloons.

After the war, *Phoenician* was rebuilt, at Government expense, and converted to a motor barge. She was sold out of trade to Albert Groom in 1949 and used for chartering before being restored and re-rigged at Maldon in 1998.

Phoenician is now owned by Grant Littler carrying out corporate entertainment work for the John F Hunt group of Grays from St. Katharine's Dock.

In the last twelve months *Phoenician* has received a new fore horse,and had work done to her decking and hold all at David Patient's Maldon yard. Further restoration work will be carried out in due course.

Phoenician took part in the Medway, Pin Mill, Blackwater and Swale events in 2012 finishing equal tenth in the Championship. It is hoped that she will compete in as many Matches as possible this year from her Maldon base.

www.johnfhunt.co.uk 01375 366888

PUDGE of Rochester

Bob - Gold wheel emblem on red & black ground. Sprit cream with blue and red bands.
Length 82.36 ft. Beam 20.98 ft. Dunkirk Little Ship.

Built 1922 by the London & Rochester Trading Co. *Pudge* worked steadily as a carrier of general cargo until being requisitioned in 1940 for "Operation Dynamo". *Pudge* was drafted to Dover and thence to Dunkirk, where, before evacuating any troops, while in tow with other barges by the Tug *St Fagan,* the latter hit a mine, the explosion is said to have "lifted *Pudge* out of the water". However, in the words of her Skipper, "She came down the right way up".

The tug and two other barges sank, but *Pudge* was towed back to England by the Tug *Tanga* laden with the survivors and three hundred servicemen.

Originally it was thought that, like other London & Rochester craft, she went to the Clyde for war duties. However research has shown that she remained trading from London to the East Coast ports, with grain and other cargos.

After the war *Pudge* continued trading as a motor barge until bought out of trade by the Thames Barge Sailing Club (now Trust) in 1968 and re-rigged to her original design for Club use. She continued in this role until 2009 when, due to lack of funds, her renovation was paused, halting her commercial sailing.

Pudge resumed sailing in 2012 following completion of her restoration and took part in the Blackwater, Thames and Swale Matches finishing overall fifteenth in the Championship. She is pictured enjoying what little wind there was in the Thames event.

www.bargetrust.org

35

REMINDER of Harwich

Bob - Green, red & white. White hull. Sprit plain cream .
Length 87.83 ft. Beam 19.38 ft.

Built of steel at Mistley in 1929 by Horlock and owned by Fred Horlock. According to tradition, she gained her name from a promise made by Fred Horlock after the 1928 Thames Barge Match, that he would "Remind" his rivals of the speed of his barges. The many successes enjoyed in Thames and Medway Matches since would suggest that this was no idle boast.

Reminder spent much of her working life transporting acid from London to the British Xylonite Plastics Ltd factory at Manningtree as well as the family trade of carrying malt and barley. She continued to carry cargos under sail until an engine was installed in 1947.

Once her career in trade was over, *Reminder* was re-rigged as a charter barge owned by Reminder (1929) Ltd and managed by Topsail Charters. *Reminder* is probably the most easily recognised of the Maldon fleet. Though used primarily for charter, she is also a fine racing barge.

Having been "Champion Barge" back in 2010, *Reminder* continues to be a regular participant in Matches appearing in the Passage, Pin Mill Blackwater and Colne events (where she won the "Golden Cockerel" award for being first over the start line) in 2012. Finishing ninth over all in the Championship.

With her white hull and the sun catching her billowing sails, Reminder makes a fine sight as she approaches Maldon Quay in April.

www.top-sail.co.uk

REPERTOR of Harwich

Staysail Class

Official No. 145404

Bob - White fish (Pollock) emblem with black 'P' on red ground. Red gunwale. Sprit cream with red banding trimmed with green. Length 86 ft. Beam 18.5 ft.

Built at Mistley in 1924 by Horlock for owners M R Horlock, *Repertor* was the first of a fleet of seven steel barges that the owner commissioned to take advantage of the extra load capacity of that form of construction. (The name "*Repertor*" means discoverer, explorer, inventor, innovator or deviser in Latin).

After a long career in trade, as a sailing barge and later as a motor tanker barge, for which role she had all her gear and deck removed and steel tanks installed, *Repertor* was sold out of trade to G Reeve and served for a time as a houseboat at Battersea.

Repertor was re-rigged by C McLaren in 1978 and is now owned by David and Elaine Pollock who operate her as a charter barge carrying twelve passengers. Usually based at St Katharine Docks, at Whitstable and at Standard Quay, Faversham. *Repertor* also operates from Maldon and other East Coast ports as required. She can be chartered from any of these locations, subject to her sailing programme. Check her website for details.

Repertor took part in all except the Southend Barge Match last year, her highlight was winning the Pin Mill Match in half a gale. She not only won the staysail class, but also beat the time of all the bowsprit barges, to win the overall pennant! She finished fourth overall in the Championship and is seen making the most of the breeze in the Medway Match.

www.repertor.com

THALATTA of Harwich

Bowsprit Class

Official No. 116179

Bob - Red with ECST in white. Length 88.9 ft. Beam 20.6 ft.

Built of wood at Harwich by W B McLearon and bought by F W Horlock *Thalatta* was launched in February 1906. Briefly spritsail rigged she was soon changed to a ketch as this was a much more suitable arrangement for the coastal and cross channel work she was carrying out.

Thalatta became a "ketch auxiliary" with a 70 hp engine when she was sold to the Wynnfield Shipping Company in 1917. *Thalatta* was sold again in 1923, this time to Herbert Body who rigged her as a spritsail barge.

Passing to R W Paul's in 1933 *Thalatta* was fitted with a diesel engine in 1947, remaining as a motor barge until, in 1967, John Kemp bought her and with Jane Benham re-fitted and re-rigged her as a "Mulie" for sail training.

Thalatta was taken over by the East Coast Sail Trust in 1971 when it was formed to provide educational cruises for children. *Thalatta* continued in this role until, with the aid of an HLF grant a refurbishment was started at St. Osyth Boat Yard in 2005, culminating in her return to service in the spring of 2012.

Thalatta competed in the Thames Match in 2012, her first race for many years. Her second place in the "Coasting Class" saw her placed equal fifteenth in the Championship. She also picked up a trophy for the fastest start and two crew awards in that event. Duties as a dedicated schools ship for ECST will determine whether or not *Thalatta* appears in any Barge Matches in 2013.

Thalatta's story is told in *"Thalatta spirit of the sea" (see P 60)*
www.thalatta.org.uk

THISTLE of London

Bowsprit Class   *Official No. 105727*   *NHSR Cert. No. 188*

Bob - Green, red & white. Grey gunwale. Sprit Light Brown, no banding.
Length 85.93 ft. Beam 22 ft.

Built at Port Glasgow in 1895 by William Hamilton and Sons, for H A Covington, a London coal merchant. *Thistle* is the oldest surviving Iron sailing barge and the only one built in Scotland to still be sailing.

Thistle spent her early life as a spritsail barge trading between the Humber and Thames with cargos of up to 150 tons of coal. By 1934 she had apparently been converted to a ketch rig as she is shown as such in that years MNL.

Thistle was sold to The London & Rochester Trading Co. in 1940. Following a mishap with her sailing gear in 1948 she was towed into Rochester where she became a motor barge when a Kelvin diesel was fitted. She continued to trade in the Thames Estuary until 1972 when she was sold to a private owner.

A number of owners had *Thistle* in the seventies and she spent some time as a houseboat. Restoration work started in 1980 when her current Gardner engine was fitted. Following a further period as a houseboat restoration was resumed and this was completed in 1987, she subsequently passed to Thistle (1895) Ltd to be operated by Topsail Charters of Maldon.

As a charter barge, she has a sailing capacity of 50 passengers, her usual charter areas are the East Coast and London and she regularly follows local Barge Matches. *Thistle* is also used for bird watching trips and other short excursions, often late in the year. She is seen here cruising the Blackwater.

www.top-sail.co.uk

VICTOR of London

Bob - White V and 1895 on dark green ground. Plain cream sprit.
Length 83.6 ft. Beam 20.30 ft.

Built of wood at the Dock End Yard, Ipswich in 1895 by Horace Shrubsall for Owen Parry. *Victor* carried linseed from East Coast farms to Parry's Mill in Colchester, then took the processed oil in drums to London. When Parry was bought out by the London and Rochester Trading Co. in 1932, *Victor* was valued at £450. Based at Chatham carrying munitions in WW2, *Victor* escaped a near miss when the lighter next to her received a direct hit from a bomb. She survived to resume her service with L.R.T.C. becoming a motor barge in 1947.

Post war *Victor* nearly met her end again when she had to be abandoned in the English Channel. Towed in to Ramsgate by the Ramsgate Lifeboat she lay unused for four years before being bought 1964 again for £450!

Her subsequent career included being a strip club and later a houseboat, until she was purchased and re-rigged in 1974 by Owen Emerson. *Victor* was sold to Nick Briggs in 1995 and used for charter work on the Solent. Acquired by Classic Yacht Charter Ltd, she underwent a major refit above and below deck in 2005/6. *Victor* is now operating out of Ipswich and Harwich but based at Mistley. Having been dry docked at Maldon over winter, *Victor* will resume her cruises in mid April.

In 2012 *Victor* only took part in the Pin Mill Barge Match, her one point giving her equal twenty first place in the Championship.

www.sbvictor.co.uk

WHIPPET
Staysail Class

Bob - Blue with white emblem. Sprit cream with blue band with white trim.

Whippet was built and worked for Humphrey and Gray, mainly in the Pool of London. She was employed as a bonded barge, holding good awaiting the payment of customs duty, re-export or movement to a bonded warehouse. which in itself makes her an extremely rare vessel.

Whippet was not powered my motor or sail but rowed or 'driven' with sweeps by a licensed waterman. The Thames Barge Driving Race founded as recently as 1975 commemorates the skills of these lightermen who moved freight on the Thames up until at least the 1930s. The 2013 event takes place on 13 July.

Purchased by Reggie Coombes in 1969, *Whippet* was maintained in working condition. later being rigged as a sailing barge and operated until the mid 1980's as, "The only iron, swim headed, lug mizzen, gaff rigged, tiller steered, topsail rigged sailing barge in the world - without an engine".

Purchased by Owen and Rita Emerson, *Whippet* has been re-commissioned with a new, conventional bow and stern and spritsail sailing rig fitted. She sometimes attends the Barge Match of her native Medway though she was only visible at her berth at Upnor again for the 2012 event.

Whippet's owners anticipate that she will be active in 2013. She is seen above pictured from Gillingham Strand on a misty morning while following the 2010 Medway Match.

WILL of Maldon

Staysail Class   *Official No. 148677*   *NHSR Cert No.234*

Photo, courtesy Topsail Events and Charters

Bob - white tower emblem on dark blue ground. Sprit plain brown.
Length 97.54 ft. Beam 24.54 ft.

One of four barges built of steel by Fellows Ltd of Yarmouth for F T Everard & Co. Ltd in 1925 as the *Will Everard.* Each barge bore the name of one of the partners in the family firm (*Alf, Ethel, Fred and Will*). These are said to have been the largest spritsail barges ever built. The *Will Everard* plied her trade round the East and South Coasts for forty years, acquiring an auxiliary engine in 1951. She was sold to a private owner in 1966 for £750 (£250 more than her original price). A condition of sale was her name could not be retained.

Under her new name of *Will* and now registered at Maldon, the barge languished on the Blackwater for two years before being resold to John Hubbins who re-rigged her and installed a new engine.

After two years as a barge yacht *Will* was sold to O.C.L. Ltd (Later P & O) who re-fitted her for corporate entertainment and promotional work. *Will* was sold in 1998 to Skipper Sue Harrison who sold her to a private owner in 2004.

Will is now operated by Topsail Events and Charters of Brighton and works mainly from St. Katharine's Dock. Able to carry up to fifty passengers on charter, her onboard facilities include PA system, multimedia projector and screen, and sound system with MP3 connection!

Compare the photograph above with the "Sprittie" *Wyvenhoe* on p 43 for a clear (if exaggerated) illustration of the shorter sprit carried on a "Mulie" rig.

www.topchart.co.uk

WYVENHOE of London

Bob - Red & white horizontal bands. Black gunwale. Name now in red. Sprit black with red/white/red banding. Length 83.93 ft. Beam 18.89 ft.

Built of steel at Wivenhoe by Forrestt & Sons Ltd in 1898, for a London owner specifically for entering Barge Matches. *Wyvenhoe* (The spelling reflects the original form of the name), was sold to the London & Rochester Trading Co. and began her life as a commercial barge in 1903. In 1923 she was fitted with her first engine and her rigging removed.

In 1982 *Wyvenhoe* was purchased and re-rigged as a company yacht barge by Wyvenhoe (London) Ltd. In 1988 she was sold to Macpherson Paints Plc who had her fitted out as a luxury yacht, lengthening her at the stern by two feet, (giving her a smaller transom) and installing a new Gardiner 6LXB diesel.

In 1992 she was sold to Charisma Consultants Limited who used her for some charter work and racing. *Wyvenhoe's* main claim to fame at this time being a bit part in the James Bond film "The world is not enough". In 2003 the company was sold to new owners and since then the barge has been Skippered and managed by Martin Phillips. The owning company was renamed Tradsail Charters Limited in January 2011.

Wyvenhoe did not take part in any Barge Matches last year though she did attend the Jubilee "Avenue of Sail". It is possible that *Wyvenhoe* will participate in Matches this year, and she continues to be available for charter.

www.wyvenhoe.co.uk

XYLONITE of Harwich

Bowsprit Class   *Official No. 145408*

Bob - White stars & tree emblem on dark blue ground. 'Avocet' emblem & Suffolk Life in topsail. Sprit grey with red bands, hull dark grey. Length 86.95 ft. Beam 18.49 ft.

Built of steel at Mistley in 1926 by F W Horlock to be named BX. after the British Xylonite Plastics Co. The company objected so she was renamed.

She carried acid for plastic manufacture from London to Brantham on the River Stour and general cargo mainly between London, Ipswich and Mistley.

Sold by Horlock's in 1958 to Greenhythe Lighterage, *Xylonite* served as a motor barge before being re-rigged in the 1970's by Tim Eliff.

Bought by the Cirdan trust in 1985, *Xylonite* was a familiar sight around the East Coast for many years operating as a charter and sail training vessel.

Sold to Rebecca Polden in 2007, *Xylonite* spent some time at Mayland having work carried out making a welcome return in 2010 with her former pale hull (see the 2009 1st edition) replaced by a stylish dark grey scheme.

Bought by photographer Tim Kent in the Spring of 2011, she spent July at Mayland for welding, then on to Faversham for further work by Tim Goldsack.

Further restoration work included hull plating and internal frame strengthening has been done and she has been completely stripped out to lighten her and make internal maintenance in the future easier. Below deck is now basic but stylish and functional. All this work meant that she was not active in 2012 but *Xylonite* will race and be available for charter in 2013.

www.xylonite.co.uk

Barges not currently active

Work in Progress

The following are undergoing major work, long term restoration or are for sale as possible restoration projects.

ATRATO of London. *Staysail Class. 'Bob' - 2 lemon diamonds on black ground.*
Official No. 110037. Built 1898 of steel. Has been static at Battersea for some years as a houseboat. N.H.S.R. List her as "Undergoing restoration".

BERIC of Harwich. *Staysail Class. 'Bob' - Dark blue & white with P in green disc on white half.*
Official No. 105421. Built of wood at Harwich 1896. Has been moved to Tim Goldsack's yard at Oar Creek for further work to be carried out.

BETULA of Ipswich. *Staysail class. 'Bob' - Plain red.*
Formerly a Dutch built bulk cement carrier later converted to a sailing barge, *Betula* is for sale at her Pin Mill base advertised as being in good condition for £98k

ENA of Ipswich.
Official No.122974 Inactive and in a sorry state at Hoo for some time, there are reported to be plans for a possible move to Pin Mill. *Dunkirk Little Ship.*

ETHEL MAUD of Maldon.
Official No. 96483. Currently undergoing restoration on the Medway.

FERTILE
SSR No 65378 former lighter now a stumpy rig swim head is currently for sale at Colchester following owner Steve Brotherhoods decision to "Come ashore" £190k fully furnished. Contact Steve on 07884 398860

GEORGE SMEED of Rochester.
Official No. 84430. Re-rigging still continues at a leisurely pace at Maldon. Sported a Christmas Tree on her topmast in December!

.GLENWAY of Rochester.
Official No. 127260. On going restoration at Maylandsea, privately owned. Dunkirk Little Ship.

HENRYof London. *Staysail Class. 'Bob'-Swallowtail with white central horizontal band on dark blue ground. Green transom.*
Official No. 118381. Built of wood at Goldsmiths yard Grays in 1904. Underwent a major refit in 2003. Based at Faversham, reportedly in poor condition being kept afloat by her pumps.

IRONSIDES of London.
Official No. 112710. Undergoing refit at Standard Quay Faversham.

LADY JEAN of Rochester. *Staysail Class.*
Official No. 148366. Built of wood by Short Brothers of Rochester in 1926. For sale (£95k) at David Patient's yard at Heybridge.

PORTLIGHT of London.
Official No. 145405. Refit at Maldon.

RAYBEL of London.
Official No. 145058. Still at Heybridge Basin for restoration work. Not yet known when this will be completed and she can return to sailing.

SEAGULL II of London.
Official No. 161348. At Gillingham where restoration continues.
TOLLESBURY of Ipswich. Having had extensive work carried out at Faversham she has now returned to Barking where her restoration continues.
VIGILANT of Harwich.
Official No. 116176 Built by Orvis and Fuller at Ipswich in 1904. Static at St Osyth for some years, she has been moved to Topsham in Devon for work to be carried out.
VIOLET of Maldon.
Official No. 96482. Stored in a lighter at Brambletree wharf near the new Medway Bridge. Waiting to be sold.
WESTMORLAND of London.
Official No. 112733. Campaign to give her a permanent base at Faversham and to get restoration properly underway seems to be making progress against those who should know better. Lottery funding being sought. Has her own Facebook page. Last of the "Brickies".

Static examples
The following are static and likely to remain so because of the nature of their use.

ARCTIC of London.
Official No: 108277, built in 1897 at Greenwich by J. Rennie.
The first fully motorised barge on the Thames and Medway when converted in 1907. Has been a houseboat for many years. Now at Benbridge, Isle of Wight.
LEONARD PIPER of London.
Official No. 129071. Built 1910 House boat at Chiswick.
WILFRED of London.
Official No. 149696. Built of steel by Piper in 1926. Currently a static nightclub at Victoria Embankment, near Waterloo Bridge.

Odds and Ends
SCONE.
Derelict and reported beyond economic repair on Benfleet Marshes.
BRITISH EMPIRE.
Very visible from the Antique Centre car park at Battlesbridge. Hulked and only partially intact, thus her internal structure is visible giving an interesting insight into the construction of a wooden Thames barge.
NORTHDOWN of London.
Official No. 148654. Built in Whitstable in 1924, She appeared as a Ketch for C. Burley, Sittingbourne in the 1934 MNL being with the same owners as Spritsail rigged in 1936. A successful racing barge in her time, she is now on exhibition at le Port Musee, Duarnenez, France. Currently under restoration, she appears in excellent external condition. A fine model of her can be seen in the Maeldune Centre In Maldon. *www.port-musee.org* nb This web site has recently been updated and no longer seems to give details of individual exhibits

Where to see the barges

The following locations regularly play host to one or more barges. Please note however that, particularly during the summer, sailing commitments may mean that they are not at home. Other locations are home to individual barges (see text) but these we have visited and can recommend.

Suffolk

Ipswich Docks
Sometimes used as a base for charter work and day trips, reasonable public access to quay.

Pin Mill
Picturesque spot, with pleasant walks along the river bank. Base for *Betula* and *Melissa*, others sometimes present.

Snape Maltings
Heritage Centre and beauty spot. *Cygnet's* usual base, sometimes has other visitors.

Essex

Maldon Quayside
Best place to see Thames barges. Home of *East Coast Sail Trust*, *Thames Sailing Barge Trust* and *Topsail Charters* and a number of private owners. Good views of the barges with easy access. *Queens Head* and *Jolly Sailor* Public Houses and *Little Ship Club* are welcoming.

Heybridge Basin
This is a good location for barges to spend the winter as they can moor in non tidal conditions and thus never "dry out". *Decima* and *Nellie* can be seen in the summer if not sailing. *Gladys* frequently overwinters in the lock and, at the time of writing, *Thalatta* is also spending the winter. *Raybel* is having work done by Tim Goldsack and can be seen behind *The Lock Tea Room*.

Kent

Faversham
Home to a number of barges and restorations, viewing not as easy as Maldon but a walk along the riverbank may give glimpses of restoration projects as well as locally based vessels.

Hoo
Limited access to view the barges in the boatyard but a number in various conditions in the area.

Whitstable
Greta and occasionally *Repertor* operate from the quay side, which makes this pleasant little town worth the visit, but check sailing schedules on websites before making a special journey!

London

St Katharine's Dock
Near Tower Bridge, this is the home of the London charter and corporate barges. A number of the "Static" example are near by.

The Thames Sailing Barge Matches

Races for Thames Sailing Barges are traditionally called "Matches" and are organised by the Sailing Barge Association. The results of the eight major Matches are used to calculate the Champion Barge for the year.

Full details of how points and classes are allocated can be found on the web site of the S.B.A. In brief they are usually as follows;

1 Point for each barge starting
1 Point for each barge finishing
3, 2, and 1 Point respectively for first, second and third in class finishers
1 Point for fastest start in class
1 Point for fastest start overall
1 Point for first past outer marker (If appropriate, there isn't one in the Passage Match)
Additional points can be awarded for seamanship.
n.b. Ten and five minute warning guns are usually fired before the start gun.

One point of interest for spectators is seeing the barges manoeuvring for position and judging their run for the start line.

Classes;
Champion Bowsprit
Fast Staysail
Slow Staysail

There are local variations on the title of these classes but these are as set out by The Sailing Barge Association. When reporting results we have used the class titles used by the event organisers.

Courses;

Except for the Passage Match, these are usually down river, round one or more buoys and back. The exact course for each event is decided by the Match Committee taking into account weather conditions on the day. Start times will depend on local tide conditions and **anyone wishing to visit a Match should check either the Match web site or that of the S.B.A before traveling.**

The Thames Match is the oldest of the Matches, being founded in 1863 by Henry Dodd, the "Golden Dustman" so called because he made his fortune collecting London's refuse! This event is said to be "The longest running, regularly organised, national racing event for traditional sail in the world".

In the following pages we list the eight Matches which go to make up the "Championship" and the dates on which they will take place in 2013. Vantage points for land based spectators have been given for each event, though without doubt the best way of viewing is from the water.

Details of vessels, including barges, available for charter for following the events are usually to be found on the individual Match's web sites which are given for convenience. Those without individual sites are linked through the S.B.A. site, *www.sailingbargeassociation.co.uk*

The full list of Barge Matches and dates for 2013

Medway

Date 2013   18 May.
Start point   Gillingham Pier
Best viewing points Gillingham Pier. Strand leisure park.
Web Site   www.medwaybargematch.co.uk
Brief history   Barge racing has taken place on the river Medway since at least 1872. Having ceased in 1914, the Matches were restarted in 1927 when the coasting class was won by Cambria! Racing ceased once more at the outbreak of WW2. In 1949 the Marina Club at Hoo organised the first of 5 matches for yacht barges, and commercial craft raced again from 1954 until the Centenary Match. The modern series started in 1965.

Results 2012

Coasting   *1st Cambria 2nd Lady of the Lea 3rd Phoenician*
Staysail   *1st Edme 2nd Repertor 3rd Decima*
Seamanship   *Lady of the Lea*

Blackwater (with Smack Race)

Date 2013   1 June
Start point   Maldon, off Osea Island
Best viewing points Stansgate sea wall, near Marconi Sailing Club. St Lawrence Bay, Bradwell.
Brief History   Organised by the Blackwater Sailing Barge Match Association which was formed in 1962.

Results 2012

Wooden-hull staysail   *1st Edith May 2nd Ardwina 3rd Pudge*
Metal-hull staysail   *1st Repertor 2nd Decima 3rd Reminder*
Bowsprit   *1st Edme 2nd Marjorie 3rd Lady of the Lea*

Passage

Date 2013   22 June
Usual start point   Gravesend to Orwell No 1 Buoy.
Best viewing points Gravesend, Southend and Walton Piers, Dovercourt.
Brief History   Inaugurated in 1978 by Blue Circle industries as the "Blue Circle Challenge Match" for a passage from Gravesend to the Orwell, usually finishing at Harwich, a distance of approximately 54 nm. The match is now organised by the Pin Mill Sailing Club.

Results 2012

One class only   *1st Edith May 2nd Repertor 3rd Ardwina*
Seamanship   *Lady of the Lea*
Fastest Start   *Edith May*

An excellent report of the 2012 Match appears on *Edith May's* web site.

Pin Mill

Date 2013	29 June
Usual start point	Butterman's Bay, near Pin Mill.
Best viewing point	River edge from Butterman's Bay Eastward. (Near "Butt and Oyster"). Shotley Marina, Harwich.

Brief History The present series of races was started in 1962 by the Pin Mill Sailing Club as an event starting and finishing at their Club.

Results 2012

Class A	*1st Mirosa 2nd Edme 3rd Marjorie*
Class B	*1st Repertor 2nd Melissa 3rd Edith May*
Class C	*1st Centaur 2nd Ardwina*
Seamanship	*Mirosa*

Thames

Date 2013	13 July
Usual start point	Gravesend, Lower Hope reach.
Best viewing point	Anchor Cove, off Royal Pier Rd, Gravesend.
Web Site	*www.thamesmatch.co.uk*

Brief History First held in 1863, twelve years after the "America's Cup" competition. Unlike that competition, the Thames Match is still contested by the same type of vessel with the same rig as when it was started and thus lays claim to being "The longest running, regularly organised, national racing event for traditional sail in the world".

This year will mark the one hundred and fiftieth anniversary of the first event and will be called the "Mark Boyle Memorial Thames Sailing Barge Match in honour of the founder of the revived series of events.

.Results 2012

Champion Bowsprit	*1st Edme 2nd Marjorie 3rd Adieu*
Champion Staysail	*1st Edith may 2nd Repertor 3rd Melissa*
Coasting	*1st Cambria 2nd Thalatta 3rd Lady of the Lea*
Seamanship	*Thalatta*

Swale (with Smack Race)

Date 2013	3 August
Usual start point	Mouth of River Swale.
Best viewing point	Sheppey shore, Harty Ferry, Shellness, Leysdown, Seasalter Shore, Sportsman foreshore, Tankerton Slopes, Herne Bay.

Brief History Organised by the Kentish Sail Association this match was first raced in 1972.

Results 2012

Bowsprit	*1st Mirosa 2nd Marjorie 3rd Lady of the Lea*
Staysail	*1st Niagara 2nd Repertor 3nd Decima*
Restricted Staysail	*1st Cabby 2nd Orinoco 3rd Phoenician*
Seamanship	*Mirosa*

Southend

Date 2013   25 August (Sunday)
Usual start point   Off Southend Pier.
Best viewing point   Southend Pier. Barges come close to the end of the
                           Pier giving an unusual view down onto them.
Web Site   *www.thamesbarge.org.uk/southendbargematch/.*
Brief History   Originally part of Southend's Regatta. The match was
revived in 1964 as one of the events celebrating the towns Golden Jubilee.
This year marks the fiftieth consecutive holding of the Match since that time.
Results 2012
Bowsprit   *Marjorie*
Staysail   *Niagara*
Seamanship   *Lady of the Lea*
                  Edith May retired
Nb The match was only contested by four barges in 2012

Colne (with Smack Race)

Date 2013   14 September
Usual start point   Between Mersea Stone and Bateman's Tower.
Best viewing point   Mersea Stone. Bateman's Tower, Brightlingsea. Barg
                           es often come very close in to Mersea Stone giving
                           excellent close ups.
Brief history   The Colne Smack Race was revived in 1971 with
Thames sailing barges invited to take part from the following year.
Results 2012
Bowsprit   *Edme*
Coasting   *Cambria*
Staysail   *Edith May*
    All barges raced as the same class with *Edme* as the overall winner, for
Championship purposes points were awarded as above for each Class.

Whitstable Harbour Day
    Although not included in the sailing barge championship, racing for tradi-
tional sailing craft takes place at the Whitstable Harbour Day each August.
Results 2012 (Thames barges only)
                  Marjorie
                  Lady of the Lea
                  Greta
                  Pudge
    The 2013 event is scheduled to take place on Saturday 3 August at the end
of the Whitstable "Oyster Festval".
Web site   *www.whitstableharbour.org*
    Greta usually features prominently in the proceedings on these occasions
and her website can be useful source of information.

Overall Championship Results 2012

Twenty four barges took part in the official championship for 2012 with *Niagara* and *Thalatta* making a welcome return after many years absence. *Pudge* was also able to participate once more following restoration work.

Champion Barge *Edith May*
Second *Lady of the Lea*
Third *Edme*

Of the vessels competing in the Championship, nine only managed a single appearance and two matches only had four competitors. Spectators wishing to see the barges in action may find the following useful;

Match	Number of barges racing
Pin Mill	16
Blackwater	11
Swale	11
Colne	10
Thames	10
Medway	7
Passage	4
Southend	4

Please remember that the numbers attending any given race can be affected by a number of non reoccurring factors, of which the weather is by far the most significant. Bad conditions or forecasts on the days preceding a Match can mean a severe reduction in the number of barges able to travel to the event. The safety of the vessels and those on board are of course paramount as is the need to avoid the unnecessary risk of expensive repairs!

The numbers given above are only for those barges racing and do not include those following the events either on charter for spectators or simply for their owners pleasure. In addition other historic vessels may also be seen following some of the Matches.

Smack Racing

Smack Racing is not organised on a championship basis in the same way as the Barge Matches, however a number of these events have Smack Races linked with them. Where this is the case we have indicated this in the calendar of matches.

A number of sailing organisations organise Smack Races and some of the more notable ones are to be found as part of the Maldon Regatta, Mersea Regatta, Whitstable and Tollesbury events.

For those wishing to know more about events featuring smacks then the web site of the Sailing Smack Association, (*www.ssa-uk.org*) publishes a list of events whilst the Colne Smack Preservation Society (www.smackdock.co.uk) is an invaluable source of information.

Smacks and Bawleys

The small fishing vessels we see competing in the Smack Races around our coast are, in very simple terms referred to as either Smacks or Bawleys.

Smack

Smack is a term meaning "Fishing boat" and is thought to originate from the Dutch "Smak" (O.E.D) derived probably from "Smakken"- to dash.(Answers.com), a logical derivation in view of their speed.

Whatever the origin of the term it is one that is applied to a variety of shapes and sizes of fishing vessels on both sides of the Atlantic. For our purposes we are concerned with the small sailing vessels primarily to be found around the East Coast of England and which are seen competing in the various Smack Races held off that coast or simply just being enjoyed by their owners on a pleasant summers day.

The excellent *Sailing craft of East Anglia* by Roger Finch and Hervey Benham, lists the following classes of smack, examples of which can still be seen today;

Leigh cockler-

Shallow craft strong and flat bottomed to withstand grounding on the hard Maplin Sands to allow the crew to spend six hours or so to rake for cockles before the turning tide covered the sand once more.

Essex oyster smack-

Finch and Benham divide these small smacks into two classes, those of twelve tons and over which were used for shrimping and stow boating (a form of fishing using a very large "fish trap" for sprats, particularly in the Thames Estuary) and the little five to twelve ton boats working the inshore oyster beds.

Essex deep sea smack-

Large vessels, sometimes up to sixty foot or more which could venture as far afield as the Dutch and Scottish coasts for fishing and to the continent of Europe when carrying cargo. Some were rigged as ketches.

Additionally, today boats specifically designed to fish for shrimps, cockles or prawns are usually referred to by the type of catch they were intended to take.

Bawley

Bawleys are defined as being transom sterned vessels with a boomless mainsail, which carried a boiler aboard for treating the catch when shrimping. This innovation greatly increased the quality of the product when it reached market. The corruption of the word "boiler" being said to give rise to the name for this class of smack.

So how can you tell the difference? In theory if the vessel you are looking at has a transom stern and no boom on it's mainsail it is a bawley and if it has an overhanging counter stern and a boom it is a smack. But, some smacks such as *Mary Amelia*, the Leigh cockler have transoms and, indeed in this case no boom and it is up to every owner how they choose to rig their boat so this can only be a guideline.

On the following pages we show some of the vessels which might be seen attending one or other of the Smack Races around our coast.

CK18 Pioneer

Built by Harris of Rowhedge 1864 Length 70 ft. Beam 15.2 ft. Berth Brightlingsea Deep sea smack with a wet well allowing it to keep fish fresh when working the Terschelling Bank off the Dutch coast - a "Skillinger smack".

CK258 Charlotte Ellen

Built by Aldous Brightlingsea 1906 Length 43 ft Berth Tollesbury This view of the pretty smack clearly shows off the counter stern typical of her type as she passes Mersea Stone at the end of a Colne Smack race.

F14 Emeline

Built 1904 by Collar of Whitstable. Length 44 ft. Berth Faversham.
A Whitstable oyster smack which was also used for shrimping, Emeline was rescued from a marina in Spain in 1992!

LO262 Helen and Violet

Built 1906 by Cann of Harwich . Length 36 ft. Berth Brightlingsea.
This pretty little bawley spent her first thirty years fishing from Leigh on Sea, she then moved to a Brightlingsea owner and has graced the River Colne ever since.

CK213 Boedicea

Built 1808 by Williamson of Maldon. Length 30 ft. Beam 10.5 ft. Berth West Mersea. Oyster smack currently based at West Mersea. Said to be the oldest boat still sailing in the world.

LO502 Mary Amelia

Built 1914 by Haywood of Leigh on Sea Length 34.95 ft. Beam 11 ft Berth Leigh on sea. A Leigh Cockler designed to land cockles from Maplin Sands.

Other vessels of interest

BARGE YACHTS

Built in 1930, *Elizabeth Anne* (above left) is now based at Tollesbury, where she is used for recreational sailing. There have been a number of these small vessels built as yachts and never intended for trade. *Blackthorn* (Not illustrated) a 44 ft vessel built in 1993 is based at Iken Cliff. Some even newer vessels are to be found on the banks of the Thames.The latest of these miniature barges is *Angela and Peter* being finished at Tollesbury. (Above right).

DUTCH BARGES   **PADDLE STEAMERS**

Dutch "Tjalk" (Roughly meaning - "like a rounded box") barges are sometimes seen round our coast and are commonly in use as houseboats. As their name implies they are of a much more rounded shape than our native barges. Most sailing today have the large boom and mast arrangement as above left on *Luctor et Emergo* seen on a visit to our waters a few years ago (above left).

There are two paddle steamers currently active, the *Waverley,* the last sea going paddle steamer in the world, and the *Kingswear Castle* (above right), the last coal burning river paddle steamer. *Kingswear Castle* is seen following the Thames Match in 2012 shortly before she returned to her home port of Dart-mouth after an absence of forty seven years!

Further reference
Web sites

www.adls.org.uk - Association of Dunkirk Little ships web site.

www.bargetrust.org - Charity dedicated to the preservation and sailing of Thames barges. Join and enjoy some sailing on *Pudge*!

www.facebook.com - Yes really! Follow the links to the SSBR page for interesting chat and pictures. Also now for Cambria and Thalatta.

www.merseamuseum.org.uk - Has Mercantile Navy Lists of various years. A fascinating glimpse into the past. Use official numbers to check barge identities as often more than one barge is listed with the same name.

www.nationalhistoricships.org.uk - National Historic Ships site. Their "Register" section is invaluable in the preparation of this book.

www.sailingbargeassociation.co.uk - Organisers of the Barge matches, Check on individual matches here.

www.sailingbargeresearch.org.uk - Home page of the Society for Sailing Barge Research. A must for the serious student of the subject especially those interested in the historical aspects.

www.thamesbarge.org.uk - Barge news.

We think that the reader will find the following publications of particular interest, all are enjoyable and some have been most useful in compiling this book.

Books

A fair wind for London - J Kemp ISBN0946547009 Reminiscences of author and founder of "Sail Trust" (Now ECST Ltd). Try the TBST for a rare copy.

Crescent Shipping. Via Thames Sailing Barge Trust. The latest offering from Ken Garrett covers over 150 years of this major sailing barge fleet operator.

Down Tops'l. Harrap, ISBN 978.0.2455066.1.1 Hervey Benham.

Last of the Sailormen. Seafarer Books, ISBN 0.7100.2024.2 R Roberts.

Mistleyman's Log. Fisher Nautical Press, ISBN 0.904340.01.5
A H & R J Horlock.

Sailing a Thames Barge, sail by sail. Via Thames Barge Sailing Trust P. Hearn. Now updated by Andrew Berry. "Which rope to pull, why to pull it what it does and when" on *S B Pudge.*

Sailing Barge Master (The story of Capt. George Winn). Chaffcutter Books, ISBN 978-0-9560596-0-4 R Walsh & D Juniper. Fascinating study of life on the barges of the late 19th and early 20th centuries. Also social history of the time.

Sailing Craft of East Anglia. Terence Dalton. 1987 R Finch & H Benham. Best history of the development of the Thames barge we have read.

The Racing Horlocks 1968-1971. (from SSBR) Ron Weyda with Bob Horlock.

The Thalatta Diaries. Heritage House (Publishing) Ltd, ISBN1.85215.1811 Rita Phillips. Amusing and entertaining account of life and work with children on a Sailing barge in the early 21st century.

Thalatta, Spirit of the sea. Phillips Design Publishing ISBN978.0.9563059.4.7 Thalatta's biography - so far!

Detail of books available from The Society for Sailing Barge Research and the Thames Sailing Barge Trust can be had from Roger Newlyn at rogernewlyn@aol.com

Definitions

The following definitions of some of the terms and abbreviations may be useful.

A.D.L.S. Association of Dunkirk Little Ships.

Bob Flag flown from main mast bearing the colours of the owner.

Brail Ropes used to furl the mains'l or mizzen. Hence to "Brail up".

Beam Width of the barge at it's widest point.

Class (Bowsprit of Staysail) used here to denote if a bowsprit is carried. Also a classification used in Barge Matches.

Ceiling Floor of the hold.

Chine Angle between the side and bottom of a barge.

Crab Small winch used for raising and lowering lee boards etc.

Depth Depth of the construction of the vessel as opposed to the amount of water she needs to float.

Draught The depth of water taken by a vessel.

Fo'c'sl (Forecastle) Space below deck in the bow which is normally used as the Mate's quarters or for storage - or both!

Gunwale (Pron. Gun'l) top of the sides of the barge.

H.L.F Historic Lottery Fund.

Horse Wood or metal beam running across the barge to which the sail is attached but free to travel from side to side.

Hatches Covers over the hold. Now often fixed.

Keelson Lengthwise member running from bow to stern which acts as the backbone of the barge.

Lighter Flat bottomed, un powered vessel for transferring cargo to and from bigger ships.

Lee board Boards carried either side of the hull and lowered on the lee (down wind) side of the barge to give added directional stability by reducing downwind drift.

Mizzen Small sail aft.

N.H.S.R. National Historic Ships Register.

Official No. Barges registration number. Useful for research purposes.

Reg.ton (Gross registered tonnage) a measure of the internal capacity of a vessel, not to be confused with the weight of cargo which can be carried. Originates from the use of "Tuns" (barrels) of wine as a measure of volume.

Sheer The upward curve to top of the hull. Barges designed for open water work have more sheer than those working rivers.

Sprit Rises at an angle from the main mast to support the sails.

Stem Bow, or Stem Post, the vertical member in the bow.

S.S.R. Small Ships Register.

Sweeps Long oars as used for the propulsion of lighters etc.

Transom Woodwork across the stern usually colourfully decorated and carrying the barges name.

Vangs Pron."Wangs". Wires to the sprit top to control its motion.

Xylonite An early form of celluloid manufactured by the British Xylonite Company. Hence the name of the barge.

Acknowledgements

It would be impossible to produce a book such as this without the assistance of a great many people. In particular the authors would like to thank all those owners, operators, skippers and crew who have contributed in various ways to this publication.

We would also like to thank Dave Brooks and Roger Newlyn for keeping us up to date with Kent based barges. John Bridgefield of Iron Wharf Boatyard, Tim Goldsack, Andy Harman and David Patience, for their updates on "Work in Progress" over the years.

We would also like to recognise the invaluable contributions by organisations such as the Society for Sailing Barge research, National Historic Ships and the Mersea Island Museum. They all need your support.

For your enjoyment

Here are a few of the other items in our range that are available. For more details contact us direct at *phillipsdesign@hotmail.co.uk*

Thalatta, Spirit of the sea   **£9.50**
ISBN 978-0-9563059-4-7

104 pages 41 colour illustrations, 25 black and white. Thalatta's "Autobiography" telling her story from first launch to refurbishment and return to sailing.

Barge Match Board Game   **£30**

This unique board game allows you to enjoy the challenges and tactics of racing your barge against the opposition and the elements.
This game is handcrafted.

Jigsaws   **£19.99**

Limited Edition 1000 piece Deluxe jigsaw of Thames Barges.

The Thalatta Diaries.   **£7.99**
Heritage House (Publishing) Ltd.
ISBN1.85215.1811

Amusing and entertaining account of life and work with children on a Sailing barge in the early 21st Century.